Very Useful Rules of English Language

English Grammar

Ariel C. Cabasag

Ukiyoto Publishing

All global publishing rights are held by

Ukiyoto Publishing

Published in 2025

Content Copyright © Ariel C. Cabasag

All rights reserved.

ISBN 9789370098275

No part of this publication may be reproduced, transmitted, or stored in a retrieval system, in any form by any means, electronic, mechanical, photocopying, recording or otherwise, without the prior permission of the publisher.

The moral rights of the author have been asserted.

This book is sold subject to the condition that it shall not by way of trade or otherwise, be lent, resold, hired out or otherwise circulated, without the publisher's prior consent, in any form of binding or cover other than that in which it is published.

www.ukiyoto.com

Acknowledgement

I truly acknowledged for publishing my English textbook. This is an indeed opportunity to work with company, where I could have shared my talents in writing, not only them but also, to the readers, who endlessly wish to acquire knowledge in English grammar. I understand that English structure can somewhat be arduous, due to proper way of using the language order in the sentences. This may not be a flawless book to guide you in writing the sentences correctly. However, this can be an impeccable book to inspire you, how imperative to engage in writing, with the integration of proper structure.

Sometimes English structure can't useful in dialogue, we admit that human beings could express the ideas freely without proper structure. However, we strongly believed that employing proper grammar could have helped us to tell the world, what we really want to be. Indeed, many speakers were able to convince people in accepting their ideas, thought it won't really acceptable to others. It's not just to be convincing, yet to use the language proficiently.

In conclusion, having a great foundation to use the language proficiently: this serves as a mirror to others, who are longing to immulate the essence of great language. To be use the language well: this inspires us to be a right bridge in the village.

Ariel's Words of Language

"Words are indeed sufficient instrument to express the ideas explicitly. However, unable to follow the appropriate rules, which might lead to confusion and misunderstanding the sentences. As non-native speakers are expected to use it incorrectly, indeed many people got confused, how to use it correctly according to the English standard. No one can be blamed such faults, however using the language through interaction or written communication, to share their thoughts. This might have helped the non-native speakers to correct their mistakes. Hence, the non-native speakers should aim to engage it, so the language can be active, which might lead to familiarization, how to apply the rules in their interaction and written communication."

"Ariel's quote"

This book consists of clear ruling, how to use the language correctly. It comprises of basic grammar, advanced, and several rules in punctuation marks. This book is useful for intermediate and proficient readers.

Author
Ariel C. Cabasag, LPT, MATELL

Published author
Research writer

Table of Contents

Basic Grammar	1
Advanced Grammar	30
About the Author	*44*

Basic Grammar

TENSE

What is tense?

It is defined as the weather or time in the sentence. In writing, this seems useful, ensuring the proper time, when something happens. Considering the proper tenses, it could have helped the readers identify what time that something has happened. To fully understand the topic, let's focus on the examples below:

Examples:

*Ralph wants to eat at **7:00 am**.*

*Ralph ate his dinner **two hours ago**.*

*Ralph will take his dinner **after** writing the assignment.*

These highlighted words are examples of tense, which show the time as Ralp did. To enlighten the brilliant minds, take time reading and identifying the tenses in the paragraph below.

To My Secret Admirer

No night is feeling awful the moment Ralph looked at her a while ago. It's indeed an imagination as he stared at the girl, however his nights pulled her, looking back the past, reuniting their image again. Over his mind," **someday, I will be meeting her again."**

Topic 1: *Using the proper tenses in the Sentences*

In English, the tense is divided into three:

Present: *The action is currently happening.*

Like for example: **Kyle writes her essay writing. She loves what she does.**

Past: *The action is done.*

Like for example: **Kyle wrote her essay writing an hour ago. She found it hard constructing the sentences, which hindered to express her thoughts explicitly.**

Future: The action will be done later or in the future.

Like for example: **Kyle will write her essay tonight.**

To further understand how to use these tenses appropriately, and when to place those mentioned tenses in the sentences. In English, there are 12 tenses, which have highlighted the different usages, constructing the sentences explicitly. Each tense does have a specific ruling. To understand its usefulness, here's first tense, along with the formula.

First tense: *Present simple tense:* **Usage**: *this tense is useful, once the writer is describing the actions that happen right now or talking about the action that happen regularly. Formula:* <u>Subject plus present main verb.</u>

Examples:

Mr. Mark talks fast.

The rainbow fades quickly.

Second tense: *Past simple action:* **Usage:** *this is useful, to describe the actions were completed in the past.* *Formula: <u>subject plus past tense of main verb</u>*

Examples:

Mark talked fast.

The rainbow faded its lights.

Third tense: *Future simple action:* **Usage:** *this is applicable, to describe prediction or expectation that will happen in the future.* <u>*Formula: subject plus future tense*</u>

Examples:

Mr. Mark will talk fast.

The rainbow will fade its lights.

Fourth tense: *Simple progressive tense: Usage: this is applicable, to describe the action is ongoing, describe plans, or temporary.* <u>*Formula: subject plus main verb+ing*</u>

Examples:

Tyler is walking on the floor.

Tyler is dreaming to become a lawyer.

Tyler is still waiting the taxi.

Fifth tense: *Past progressive tense:* **Usage:** *this is useful, to describe the action seems interrupted, simultaneous, and emphasizing the point.* **Formula:** <u>*subject plus past action+ing.*</u>

Examples:

Tyler was playing while the mother called his attention.

Tyler was eating while Carl was studying.

Sixth tense: *Future progressive tense:* **Usage**: *this is useful when someone refers to emphasize that the action will happen over a period of time. Formula: <u>subject plus future action+ ing</u>*

Examples:

Ms. Queen will be waiting the submission date at 7:00pm.

Ms. Queen will be sending her response before twilight.

Seventh tense: *Present perfect tense:* **Usage**: *this is useful when someone describes actions that started in the past, and are still relevant to the present. Formula: <u>subject plus has/ have plus past participle.</u>*

Examples:

Ms. Cartel has watched the news for an hour.

Ms. Cartel and Ms. Kyle have spent their vacation, since December 2024.

Eight tense: *Past perfect tense:* **Usage**: *this is useful, when someone describes a past that happened before another past event. Formula<u>: subject plus had plus past participle.</u>*

Examples:

Angelo had fallen his tears before Carrol loved him.

Angelo arrived the classroom, the teacher had already started the class.

Nine tense: *Future perfect tense:* **Usage:** *this is useful, when someone describes an action that will be completed before a specific time in the future. Formula: subject plus will plus have*

Examples:

My mother is already in the house. I will have cleaned the floor this time.

In time of summer, Ariel will have enjoyed his vacation.

Tenth tense: *Present perfect continuous tense.* **Usage:** *this can be used correctly, once someone aims to describe an action that began in the past are still happening in the present. Formula: subject plus have/ has plus been*

Examples:

Earl has been hiding his secret admirer since, 16 years old till now.

Earl and Joshua have been studying Juris doctor for more than five years.

Eleventh tense: *Past perfect continuous tense:* **Usage:** *this is applicable when someone describes action that started in the past, and still happening when another event occurred. Formula: subject plus had plus been plus ing*

Examples:

Piolo had been reading the books for six hours, before he understood the texts.

By the time, Ariel and Piolo had been taking their lunch together, it's a perfect moment completed their nights.

Twelve tense: *Future perfect continuous tense:* **Usage**: *this is applicable when someone describes an action that will be completed before a specific time in the future, and to emphasize the length of action. Formula: subject plus will plus has/have plus ing.*

Examples:

By January 2025, Jamella will have been learning the research paper for several weeks.

Kate will have been working for eight hours, as Ellie arrives in the mansion.

Piolo and Ariel will have have been talking for a night before Angel comes.

VERBS

It is defined as the action word in the sentence. Throughout its presence, it does help to emphasize the behavior or actions in the sentence. Considering the essential part of the action word, which leads to better understanding, how someone or something does really work. To classify the verbs and understand, when to use it, and where to place it specifically in the sentences.

Link verbs: **(is, are, was, & were)**

The mentioned verbs are applicable, when someone refers to connect the subject and verb in the sentences. Like the examples below:

Piolo is taking his rest.

Piolo and Heinrich are dreaming to become rich.

Piolo was cooking while Kyle called his attention.

Piolo and Paulo were friends in the University.

Note: *The mentioned verbs can be used to ask questions. Like for example," Is Piolo taking his rest?" "Were Heinrich and Piolo dreaming about their ambition in life?" In addition to that, the verb should follow after the subject. However, if it refers to questions; hence, it might have appeared in the beginning before the introduction.*

Auxiliary/Helping verbs: **(have, do, has, does, will, &did)**

The mentioned verbs are applicable, once the readers have desires to clarify the meaning of the action, which has expressed by the main verb in the sentences. Like the examples below:

Heinrich has sent his email for an hour.

Heinrich does remain silent while Ariel doesn't.

Heinrich and Ariel have taken their vacation at Virgin island for a month.

Heinrich will take his lunch later.

Heinrich did his part as a full-time faculty.

Note: *This wouldn't limit on how to use it in the sentence, however it could be used in asking questions. Like for example,"* **did Heinrich do his part as a full-time faculty?" "Will Heinrich take his lunch later?" and Have Heinrich and Ariel been taking their vacation at Virgin island for a month?"**

Topic 2: Important parts of the Sentences

PARTS OF THE SENTENCE

1. Subject
This refers to the main topic in the sentence. This can be identified either person, thing, animal, and object in the sentence. To fully comprehend the function and usage, here's an example below.

Mariane takes time reviewing her notes before going to school.

2. Predicate
This refers to the verb which shows an action in the sentence. This could be placed after the main topic, to highlight the action. To understand better, here's the example below.

Alvin travels to Manila at 10:00am.

3. Direct Object
This refers to the word which receives the action. This can be found beside the verb. Like for an example:

Mariane saw scary snakes beside the river.

4. Subject Complement
This refers to noun or adjective which further modify the subject. Like for example:

Piolo is ravishing man at Far Eastern University.

Topic 3: Essential elements of Speech

BASIC PARTS OF SPEECH

Ruling:

1. Noun

This defines as the name of people, things, animals, places, and objects. This can be found anywhere in the sentences. To identity those mentioned names, asking these ***Wh-questions; what, where, when, which, and who,*** which could have helped to find the noun in the sentences. These are the examples below:

Piolo has been appearing his image for a night. *(That sentence, asking question; what is applicable for us locating the noun)*

Every smile can be found on the island.

Valentines day is the best moment to remember my past *(That sentence, asking question; when is the best question for us to locate the noun)*

2. Pronouns

This refers to the word which can be used to substitute the noun. This helps to minimize the repetition of the noun. Like for example:

Kyle is a lovely man that I ever met in life. However, two years passed he seemed sarcastic and ill-mannered.

To discuss further the pronoun consists of three cases; subjective case, objective, and possessive case. Each of them is useful in writing the sentences. Well, let us define the usage on those cases.

2.1 Subjective (I, you, he, she, we, & it)

This refers to indicate the subject in the sentence. Like for examples;

You have sent the file through MS teams.

He will make the class alive entire period.

She can take care of it.

It takes a year of seeing her again.

The subjective case can be found in the beginning of the sentences. However, it might be placed after in the middle and end.

2.2 Objective (me, him/her/us/them/whom

This refers to the pronoun that acts as subjects in a sentence. To fully understand the usage, these are the examples below.

I can't touch **her** again.

I saw **him** over my dreams last night.

Let **us** make the class meaningful.

Just keep on motivating **them**.

The mentioned case can be found usually after the verb. This is essential, due to mentioned specific actions.

2.3 Possessive (mine, yours, hers, his, theirs, & ours)

This refers to the pronoun which shows the relationship and ownership in the sentences. To completely understand the usage and function, these are the examples below:

Heinrich as live the heart as forever mine.

She couldn't the kingdom, due to hers palace.

3. Preposition

This refers to connect the noun, pronoun, and clauses in the other words within a sentence. This can be found usually beside the verb, before the pronoun, and before the noun.

PREPOSITION

Preposition, a part of speech acts as connector between noun and another words in the sentences. In English, it plays a crucial role, which does have helped the words, connecting the thoughts together. Like for example, the bird is flying under the tree. As noticed the word," under" wants to connect the bird to tree. To further comprehend the usage of preposition. Let us study the ruling:

Rule #1: *The preposition should contain an object. The sentence should have preposition, otherwise it can be considered as adverb. To understand the ruling,*

Ariel is in the mall.

Ariel takes his lunch after the game.

Ariel wants to answer the test before the exam.

Rule # 2: *The preposition must be placed before the noun. This can be placed before the noun or pronoun. To understand the ruling, these are the examples below:*

Hannah will meet her friend in the park.

Hannah might be late in the afternoon.

Rule # 3: *The pronoun following the preposition should be act as object. This is very useful, let's learn the given examples below.*

The sun was from the sky.

The star is between the lakes and mountain.

Rule # 4: *Don't confuse preposition "to" with infinitive to, in and into. Let's see the examples below.*

I look forward to meeting you soon.

I love to dance beside her.

To completely understand the concept, let us categorize the prepositions below.

Common prepositions:

On- This can be used in the sentence, as someone refers to indicate date, position along a line, or on a surface. Like example:

> *The visitor is waiting on the street.*
>
> *Rick will win the lotto on Friday.*
>
> *She puts the glass on the table.*

At- This can be used as preposition, as someone would like to connect the word specifically; location, time, activities, numbers, and direction. Like for examples:

I will sleep at 7:00pm.

My work is beside at Far Eastern University, Marikina City.

I am not good at dancing.

In-This can be used as preposition: this refers to connect the words generally. Like for examples:

She will be staying in my heart.

I live in Quezon City.

Of- This can be used as connectors, once the intention is to show the relationship between people or things. Like for example:

Which of the objects do you like?

Let my warmful regards of her.

Is she the model of Nice island?

For- This is very useful as connectors, once someone does have an intentions to indicate duration of time, purpose, reason, and recipient. Like for examples:

Ariel bought a jacket for him.

Tyler might finish the activity for a month.

ADJECTIVES

It is defined as the color and descriptor in the sentences. This can be found specifically before or after the noun in the sentences. Here, this plays as a vital role providing a clear description, what the noun is all about. To comprehend the usage and its usefulness, here's the following examples:

*The **wonderful** aircraft fell down in the mountain.*

*Ariel takes an hour reading the **difficult** cases.*

*The king finds his **spectacular** dreams under the tree.*

The adjectives can be found anywhere in the sentences. It can be easy to find the adjectives, which modify the noun or pronoun in the sentences. It can be displaced in the beginning, middle, or in the end. To further understand the ruling, these are the following rules below:

Order: *opinion, size, physical quality, age, color, origin, material, type, and purpose*

ADVERB

Adverb is part of speech that describes the noun, adjectives, and another adverbs. It usually answers how, when, where, why, and what. Asking those questions, the readers could easily identify the adverb in the sentences. To clearly understand, the function of the adverb: to modify or provide an expansion, what the sentences would like to tell to the readers. Some readers often got confused, how to use it clearly, especially non-native speakers, however it could easily find the appropriate adverb in the sentences. To further comprehend the usage, let us understand the rules below.

Rule 1: *Many adverbs end in -ly, but many do not. Generally, if a wonder can have -ly added to its adjective form, place it there to form an adverb.*

Examples:

Kate writes her thoughts quickly.

She usually wears her favorite t-shirt.

Rule 2: *Adverbs can be found after the linking verb, asking wh-question. This really helps to locate the adverb in the sentences. To clearly understand the sentences, these are the following examples below:*

Kyle's eyes looked mad at her.

Seeing the bay, Kyle smells the sweet fruit quickly.

Rule 3: *The word good is an adverb whose equivalent is well. This word can be placed after the linking verb or after the phrase. Like for examples:*

The doctor advised me to visit in the clinic, to get well.

The physician didn't report his office, unless his health might be well.

Note: *If it refers to health, on the other hand, well take as an adjective. Like for example:*

The physician does feel well today.

Rule 4: *Adjectives come in three forms, called degrees; positive, comparative, and superlative. This might come anywhere in the sentences either middle or ending. To understand the ruling, these are the examples below:*

Piolo is a sweet man.

Piolo is sweeter than Paulo.

Piolo is the sweetest men in the village.

Rule 5: *Don't drop the -ly from an adverb when using the comparative form. To comprehend the ruling, these are the examples below:*

Allen is wealthier than Alvin. He moves quicker than him.

I find it easier than before.

Rule 6: *The demonstrative pronouns; this, that, these, and those are followed by a noun, they are adjectives. However, if those mentioned pronouns appear without a noun, they are pronouns. To fully understand the examples:*

This woman is currently employed in London.

Those men are sarcastic in the office.

CONJUNCTIONS

Conjunction, *a part of speech acts as a joiner between phrases and sentences. The main function is to connect the words together. Like for example, you have been loving her for a thousand years. The connector is the word," for" next to the next phrase, which does help to complete the meaning.*

In writing the sentences, **FANBOYS***; for, and, nor, but, or, yet, and so are common. However, as non-native speakers can commit mistakes both writing and speaking. To use them appropriately, let's define the usage, including their applicability in the sentences.*

FOR- *This is applicable in the sentences, if the intention is to state the purpose, reason, indicate the year. This seems useful writing, especially when the writers or speakers would like to intend the purpose or reason for someone else or something. Like for examples:*

Earl James kept on working at night shift for his family.

Earl James wrote a letter for making his mind awake.

Earl James has been loving his girlfriend for a year.

AND- *This is applicable if the intention is to combine the ideas together in the sentences. The common reason why the ideas* *should need to combine, using and, so the ideas can be stated concisely. In addition to that, the writer should use and: to suggest something, which merely valuable for the expansion of the ideas. Like for examples:*

Earl James & Angel have shared their hearts together.

Earl James walked on the floor, and turned his eyes on the ground.

NOR- *This is applicable if the intention is to indicate that something is not true, possible, or allowed. This word simply means that the two statements are negative, which can't be true. Like for examples:*

Neither Earl James nor Jazzmen I like.

She loves cooking nor watching movies.

BUT. *This is applicable if the intention is to indicate the connection the contrasting ideas. The word simply pointed out that, if the writer or speaker wants to contrast the ideas simply. Well, this conjunction is very useful. Like for examples:*

Allen wants to stay motivated all the time, but his family demotivated him the most.

Allen does have a desire to mingle his friends, but the time is insufficient.

OR. *This is applicable if the author's intention is to indicate the choices between the two options. It's useful either formal or informal language. To completely understand the usage, these are the following examples below.*

Xavier wants to take his break or socialize with his friends.

Xavier is till undecided either to leave the country or stay his loved ones.

YET. *This is applicable if the author's intention is, to indicate that something hasn't happened up to the present time. This can be usually placed at the end of the sentences. Let's us exercise the usage of* **yet** *in the sentences below. Like for examples:*

Lance hasn't yet arrived.

The manager had ended the call yet.

SO. *This is applicable, if the author's intention is to indicate the result, consequence, and to conclude something. This is very useful in writing both academic writing and actual communication, especially when the author's intention is, to connect the clause. To completely understand the ruling, these are the examples below:*

Ariane hasn't successfully passed the exam, so she spends more time reading her books.

Ariane lets them know what to do, but they didn't understand her. So, Ariane utters the words slowly.

ARTICLES

Article is defined as an adjective in the sentences, which can be usually placed before the noun. It's easily to identify the article: however, it can be difficult to place it accurately. In general ruling, the article seems relevant beside the noun, which demonstrates whether the noun seems specific or general. Moreover, the article can be categorized into two, a/an is used once the main point is general, the, on the other hand, is used once the main point is specific.

To fully comprehend the usage of indefinite article, let us focus on the ruling below:

Rule 1: If a/an is used the noun modified is indefinite, which generally refers to any member of a group.

Ariel wants to buy a dog.

Someone calls a man.

When I climbed in the mountain, I saw an eagle.

As what we have noticed, the noun is being modified, it wasn't specific. Hence, a/an is used in the examples above.

Rule 2: To use a/an depends on the sound that begins the next word. In short, before deciding what noun is appropriate, it's important to check the sound before placing it beside the noun.

a teacher

an eagle

an umbrella

a man

Rule 3: If the noun is being modified by an adjective, the choice between a and an, which merely depends on the initial sound of the adjective that immediately follows the article.

a broken man

a pretty woman

Rule 4: The indefinite article used as to indicate membership in a group or organization. To fully understand, let us see the examples below.

I am a member of KPB ng Pilipinas.

Kyle is a British national.

Note: If there's an indefinite article, there's also definite article. It can be placed before singular/plural nouns, when the speaker or writer takes the noun as particular. To fully comprehend the usage, let us check the examples below.

Rule 1: The definite article can be considered as noncount noun in the sentences. Let us remember the uncountable nouns, so we could used what article to be used. Let us check the examples below:

I love watching the clouds.

Kyle used the vinegar to his viand.

Rule 2: The definite article can't be used before most countries or territories.

General rule: The definite article can be used before the specific noun. Otherwise, the indefinite can be used wisely.

Basically, the parts of speech is essential before proceeding to the ruling. Having the knowledge on the mentioned guidelines is indeed a prerequisite before moving to the context. Now, let us move forward on the general ruling, how to use the verb and subject properly.

Rule 1: The singular subject should align with singular verb.

Jeremy shares his time with Ana.

Khant takes her time reviewing the test papers.

Rule 2: To use present perfect tense, all singular subject used has, plural used have in the sentence.

She never had carried the sack.

The wind and rain have fallen on the sea.

Rule 3: To use the compound subjects, both of them should be combined using the conjunction, using and.

The beautiful lawyer and ugly teacher have proven their feelings till the end of the year.

Ana and Allen were attending the mass yesterday.

Rule 4: When more than subjects, to use the appropriate verb. You should choose the subject nearest to the verb.

Bake, sandwich, or grape is my favorite food.

Gift or love is the best value in the hierarchy.

Rule 5: Indefinite pronoun always takes singular

Everyone is on the stage.

Nothing makes me okay.

Nobody loves me, except my parents.

Rule 6: Either or neither nor, the verb should agree with noun or pronoun that comes before it.

Either the lawyer or the doctor is the best.

Neither the teacher nor the principal agrees the penalty.

Rule 7: The subject seems plural in form, but the usage is singular.

The news seems interesting, unlike before.

Physics is my favorite subject in life.

Rule 8: Interrogative sentence is concerned, the first verb (be verb or do verb) has to be aligned with the subject of the sentence.

Do you read romantic novels?

Does she like it?

Is Earl a good man for her?

Were you checking the manuscript?

Rule 9: The sentence begins here, there, this, that, those, & these, etc. The demonstrative should be treated as subject in the sentence.

There were ten men, who hid beside the wall.

That was a wonderful tale.

Rule 10: Uncountable noun and countable noun should always take as singular subjects.

Values Education is important in the curriculum.

Love makes me happy to see him again.

Rule 11: Time, distance, or money takes as a singular verb in the sentence.

200 billion US dollars is worth it.

1 Million kilometer takes a year

Rule 12: The collective noun as the subject of the sentence, the verb can be singular or plural based on the context.

Cabasag family is feeling satisfied in UK.

All of the club members shared their different insights about the impeachment.

Rule 13: All, some, and few take as plural form in the sentence.

All of students are unresponsive today.

A few of my books have gone in the mini library.

Rule 14: Sentence begins with each or every, as the subject. It always takes as singular verb.

Each of the student has an assigned committee.

Every man deserves to be loved.

Rule 15: Expressing a wish or request, the verbs are used a little differently from other sentences.

I wish I were an eagle.

If you were here, I wouldn't be sarcastic.

Note: The mentioned SVA above is useful writing the sentences, including daily conversation. As non-native speakers, grammar can be used incorrectly. However, it's important to remember, to use the standard ruling.

Topic 4: Essential parts of Antecedent

ANTECEDENT

Ruling of antecedent pronoun

Let us defined the meaning; **antecedent** is a word for which a pronoun stands. If SVA is essential in writing and speaking, pronoun is also important to consider both writing and speaking. Like for example, *"Earl James wants to prove his secret tales before twilight."* Upon checking the example, the word "his" refers to the man, who wants to prove something. To completely understand the usefulness of antecedent, let us follow the rulings below:

Rule 1: A phrase or clause between the subject and verb doesn't change the number of antecedents. To fully comprehend the usage, let us check the examples below.

The flower gives its wonderful smell.

The ravishing man shows his talents in the show.

Rule 2: A singular indefinite pronoun antecedents take singular pronoun referents. To fully comprehend the ruling, let us check the examples below.

Everybody gets ready for the final presentation.

Someone really takes into my heart.

Exceptions:

Plural indefinite pronoun antecedents require plural referents like several, few, both, and many

To know the usage, let us check the examples below:

Several bar takers take their serious review.

Many of the gifts are useful in the Valentine's day.

Rule 3: Compound subjects joined by and always take a singular referent. To fully comprehend the usage, let us check the examples below.

Ariel and Earl have shared their lovely nights.

The bird and cow are examples of wonderful creatures.

Rule 4: The collective nouns (group, crowd, team, etc.) may be singular or plural depending on the meaning.

The members of the club share their different concerns, regarding the political issues.

The crowd affects the traffic today.

Rule 5: The titles of single entities; books, organizations, countries, etc.) take a singular referent.

The Story of Kies gives its meaningful application in life.

The movies is better than the books.

Rule 6: The number of vs a number of before a subject: To simplify, the number of takes as singular, while a number of takes plural.

The number of VP's supporters is uncountable.

A number of promises are enough.

Topic 5: Worth to remember the essential parts of Punctuation marks

PUNCTUATION MARKS

Ruling of Punctuation Marks

Punctuation mark serves as the symbols in the sentences. Basically, it functions as signal, **which does have helped to divide the phrases and sentences**. Without considering the PM, the thoughts may be affected which leads to confusion. To completely understand the ruling, let us categorize the rules below.

Commas (.). This refers to the symbol, which can be used to separate ideas or phrases. This plays as a vital role in the sentences. To completely understand, let us follow the examples below:

One of the memories that I can't forget is farewell. No other word is important than love.

The family shows its love and compassion to each member. However, love might turn into hatred once everyone doesn't support to each other.

Apostrophes ("). This refers to the symbol, which can be used effectively, ***to indicate possession or contraction.*** To completely understand the usage, let us observe the examples below.

We won't love you, unless you come again.

The woman's eyeglass has reminded us to be strong.

Quotation Marks ("). This refers to the symbol, which can be used effectively, **to highlight the main point of the sentences**. To completely understand the usage, let us observe the examples below.

The poem,***" often loving you***," is the best literary works that I ever had written.

One of the best stories I read,***" Chain of Poetic Tales,"*** which reminds me to keep loving my past.

Colons (:) This refers to the symbol, which can be used effectively, ***to show the emphasis, present the dialogue, business letter, explanation, and introduce the information***. To completely understand the usage, let us observe on the given examples below.

Earl James took his study seriously: he wanted to give fruit his labor.

Dear Sir Earl:

These are the following students, who have passed the contest:

Semicolon (;) This refers to the symbol, which can be used to separate two independent clauses; ***without a conjunction and without a conjunctive adverb***. To comprehend further, let us observe on the given examples below.

She wants to travel today; however, the weather seems awful.

Dave returns the letter; it contains the hatred.

Ellipses (…) This refers to the symbol, which can be used to indicate the words, which have been omitted from quote. To completely understand the ruling, these are the rules below:

The meeting may start…

I wanted to let you know why I left the Group chat, however …

Advanced Grammar

Basic rules are essential in writing essays, dialogues, and speeches. Let us accept the fact that incorrect grammar is inevitable in writing and speaking. Nevertheless, frequent engagement is commendable, to retain the rules in our brilliant minds. Acquiring that knowledge, it helps us to be confident in expressing the ideas through writing and speaking. To acquire more learning, how to use the language proficiently, let us engage the advanced ruling, though advance grammar is applicable for writers and native speakers, still as non-native speakers, it's more than a requirement to continuously learning the language. Having a sufficient learning, it could have helped us clearly comprehend the connotation of literary works like novels, memoir, and essays, including the native speaker's conversation. Knowing the fact that incorrect grammar might have changed the meaning, due to the inorganize syntax.

Understanding the correct usage of advanced grammar seems challenging as non-native speakers. However, being committed on how to use the rules appropriately, it could have helped us to make it easy, which could lead to a better grammar. Let's remember that incorrect grammar is unavoidable as non-native speakers, however it could be strengthened through constant practice, till miracle happens. Are you waiting for the miracle? Someday, you will be astonished, how miracle may happen in your writing skills.

-Ariel-

To fully comprehend how advance grammar embedded the language, let us observe the ruling and examples below.

CONDITIONAL SENTENCES

Conditional defined as hypothetical situation and its possible results. Knowingly that **conditional usually begins with "if".** *Let us categorize the usage conditional sentences, along with its usefulness in the reality.*

ZERO CONDITIONAL. *This is applicable when someone tells about the truth, scientific facts, and general habits. If the situation seems happy in reality. To fully understand the usage, let us observe on the given examples, along with the formula, if it has been applied or not.*

Topic 1: Conditionals

Formula: If + present simple= subject + present simple

If I am tired, I watch movie.

If I walk the stage, I feel confident.

FIRST CONDITIONAL. *This is applicable when someone refers to realistic situation; this can be relatable in life. To fully comprehend the usage, let us apply the formula: If + present simple = will + verb or imperative form.*

If you were sad today, I will buy a gift.

If you feel happy, I will treat you a dinner.

SECOND CONDITIONAL. *This is applicable when someone refers to impossible situation that may have happened in the future. To understand the usage, let us apply the formula: if + past simple= would/ could verb form.*

If I were you, I would buy a gift.

If I were you, I would stay in London.

THIRD CONDITIONAL. *This is applicable when someone describes the regrets. To completely understand the usage, let us observe examples, along with the formula: if + past perfect= would have/could/must + past tense.*

If I had attended the party, I would have met my friends before dying.

If I had taken his heart, I might have enjoyed my life on Valentine's day.

RELATIVE CLAUSES

This refers to the helping hand of noun or pronoun in the sentences. This usually comes anywhere in the paragraph. Basically, the task or function is to provide more information about the noun or pronoun. Always take note, these relative clauses can be placed anywhere in the paragraph.

These are the relative clauses below:

Who. *This question answers the name of person or animals. To fully comprehend the function of who, let us observe on the examples below.*

The beautiful girl, who wears a green t-shirt, keeps on appearing over my eyes.

Ms. Allen runs at the back of Kyle, who seems protective and elegant.

Which. *This question refers to specify about a particular person, place, or things. To completely understand the function of which, let us check the example.*

Mr. Romel checks his expenses, which makes him irritated.

I wanted to know the cause of his illness, which might end my pain.

Whose. *This question does have helped to provide further about the ownership. This is useful, especially when someone is trying to emphasize the ownership. Let us check the specific examples below.*

I saw a woman whose dog danced with her.

May I know whose mother is sleeping on the floor.

That. *This question points out about something. This is useful, especially when someone attempts to point out essence of noun.*

I can carry Alvin's bag; however, that day seems satiric.

That contribution might make me feel better.

When. *This question could provide an information about the time. This seems relevant to use in the sentences, especially when someone refers to the time.*

Teddy attends the party, when the contribution seems budget-friendly.

I don't want to be there, when my enemy attends the occasion.

Where. *This question could provide an information about the place. This is very useful, when someone wants to specify further about the place.*

I often dreamt to stay in London, where I might meet my dream man. I don't want to publish my book in USA, where I encountered scam publishers.

Why. *This question could provide an information about reason. This is very useful, when the speaker wants to state the reason about something. To completely understand, let us observe on the given examples below.*

My friend stopped her studies, due to financial problem.

Eric doesn't want to show his feelings: to avoid misunderstanding.

Topic 2: Modals

PERFECT MODALS/PAST MODALS

Perfect modals used **to describe the possibility, certainty, ability, regret, and more in the past.** These modals might appear usually after the adjective in the sentences. To enlighten our minds, regarding the usefulness of modals in daily conversation. let us observe the ruling below.

Could have: *This could be used if something was possible in the past; it didn't happen.* This is relatable in life, especially when someone wishes to do something for him/her. Let us check the examples below:

I could have expressed my secret to her, but I surrendered to let her know.

Let us compare to: ***could have been***; possibility in the past that didn't happen.

I could have been expressing my secret, but I changed my mind for a second.

Would have: This could be used if the unfulfilled intention in the past or to express regrets, wishes, or opinion. This seems relatable, as human beings might regret, due unfulfilled wishes that we wanted to let them know.

I would have met her, Ariel has gone.

Let us compare to: would have been; to convey a sense of regret or longing for something that didn't happen.

I would have been meeting him; hypothetically, something won't be the perfect for.

Should have: This is useful *to express the regret or criticism about something that didn't happen in the past.* Like for example:

I should have sent the love letter, but the network seems bad. In contrast to the other: should have been means to express something that was expected to happen but didn't happen. This seems relatable to life, there's a time to keep on expecting on something, due to some considerations, it won't happen.

I should have been sending the love letter for three times, but internet makes it failed.

Must have been: This is useful to express high degree of certainty that didn't happened in the past.

I *must have been* attending the mass for half-day, but the rain never stopped.

Topic 3: Importance of Speeches

-DIRECT SPEECH-

It's a form *of speech where the speaker states the message itself.* It's commonly happening in the daily conversation, especially in business world. This can be relatable in life, human beings crave to quote information from someone else, to highlight the importance of the statement. Let us follow on the general example below.

"Productive county does have a unity," Lance said.

As we have noticed that the statement has been explicitly stated by Lance. It's indeed clear to understand Lance's opinion about the productive country. Let us put in mind that direct speech does have speakers, who utters the message not the receiver. On the other hand, indirect speech means the act of repeating something was said, but really the same words. This may usually happen, especially when someone wants to rely the information to someone else. Let us observe the example below.

He said that he always came late to his class.

He said he wanted to surrender his problems, due to financial stability.

To further develop the understanding, let us check the ruling below:

RULE 1: *Direct speech is in past tense then all present tenses are changed to the corresponding past tense in indirect speech.*

Direct Speech: He said," I am happy."

Indirect Speech: He said that he was happy."

RULE 2: ***The tense of direct speech do not change if the reporting verb is in the future.***

Direct Speech: He says," I am walking on the way."

Indirect Speech: He says she is going.

The present perfect changes to past perfect.

Direct Speech: "I have been to London," Mauro said.

Indirect Speech: She told me that he had been to London.

If it's present continuous changes to past continuous

Direct Speech: "I am watching the movie," Noel said.

Indirect Speech: Noel said that he was watching the movie.

If it's simple present changes to simple past

Direct Speech: I am not feeling well.

Indirect Speech: She said that she was not feeling well.

RULE 3: *If the tense is simple past changes to past perfect.*

Direct Speech: Earl said," Marl visits the apartment on Sunday."

Indirect Speech: He said that he Marl had visited on Sunday.

Note: Past continuous changes to past perfect continuous.

Direct Speech: "We were meeting in the campus," they told me.

Indirect Speech: They told me that they had been meeting in the campus.

Note: future changes to present conditional

Direct Speech: I will be in Qatar next week.

Indirect Speech: She said that she would be in Qatar, next week.

Note: future continuous changes to conditional continuous

Direct Speech: He said," I will be discussing the research method next day.

Indirect Speech: He said that he would be discussing the research method next day.

Topic 4: Essential parts of phrases

PHRASE

It's a group of words which doesn't have a complete thought. There is an absence of subject and verb in the sentence. There merely appear in the paragraph, which seems thoughtless. Like for examples," *in the afternoon, of the night, and bore on."* To further know the other types, let us elaborate more about it.

Noun phrase

It's a group of words that contain noun, which used to modify. Generally, it functions as subject, object, or complement. It can be complicated to act as noun phrase, yet it might be easier to find for it.

My boyfriend's sister had come late from the school.

The students were tasked to **seek the paper.**

ADJECTIVE PHRASE. It's a group of word that contains adjective, which functions to complement. In short, the function of AD is to provide more information about noun. Like for example:

Angelo has white *complexion, cute, and sweet smile*.

People, *in the village*, often feel crazy.

ADVERB PHRASE. It's a group of words that includes an adverb and other modifiers. It can be found anywhere in the sentence. Like for examples:

In the night, my friend will start his project.

They went to the town at the park.

VERB PHRASE. It's a group of words that can be used like a verb. Generally, it consists of a main verb and auxiliary verb. Like for examples:

Mike has been waiting for his order.

Miguel is taking his dinner.

PREPOSITIONAL PHRASE. It's a group of words which consist of preposition and object. This can be found anywhere in the sentence. Let's see the examples below:

Sittie wants to work with the lovely man.

On the floor, everyone is not allowed to pass by.

INFINITIVE PHRASE. It's a group of words which begins with infinitive like "to" plus a verb. This can be usually placed in the beginning. Like for examples:

To love you is like a rain.

We wanted to ran away.

GERUND PHRASE. It's a group of words, which begins a gerund and any modifiers or objects. The word usually ends with -ing in the sentences. Like for examples:

Walking on the road is my challenge.

One my best dreams to staying with you.

APPOSITIVE PHRASE. It's a group of words that renames or defines a noun in the sentence. Like for examples:

My boyfriend's car, a new model, is one the best vehicles that I found.

The teacher, an extraordinary talented girl, will end his service this month.

Topic 5: Essential parts of Clauses

CLAUSES

It's a group of words which contain subject and verb. The statement does have presented complete thoughts, however it couldn't consider a full of grammatical sentence. Basically, the clause consists of types:

Independent clause: *It's a group of words with a subject and verb, which does help to completely stand alone. To completely understand the context, let us observe the examples below.*

I wanted to let him know about my interest, but he kept on ignoring my presence.

I am happy to meet my family again; however, I feel sad to see my father, who got sick.

Let us check on the given examples above. The sentences could stand alone because of the subject and verb. However, due to the conjunction, it would make the sentence hanging. Despite that, the thought is still highlighted, with the help of subject and verb.

Dependent clause: It's a group of words which can't stand alone, due to lack of additional information. The mentioned group of words often depend on the independent clauses to clearly express the ideas. Let us observe on the given examples below:

When I wrote the story

Although the night seems better

Let us check on the given examples, the thought was incomplete. To express it clearly, the sentence should need to expand, however independent clause will be utilized.

Topic 6: Worth to remember the voices

VOICE

This indicates the connection between the subject and object of a sentence. It signifies whether the subject acts or receives the action.

RULE 1: Identify the subject +verb+object in the active sentence to convert to passive voice.

Like for example:

Marriane carry the ***bag***.

RULE 2: Interchange the object and subject with each other.

Example:

Marriane carry the bag. (active)

The bag was carried by Marriane. (passive)

RULE 3: In passive voice sometimes, the subject is not used, the passive voice can be deleted without enough meaning.

Example:

Friel is in the bar.

RULE 4: Change the base verb in the active sentence into the past participle (by, with, to, etc.)

Example:

Mark Justin painted the wall.

The wall was painted by MJ.

RULE 5: Use the suitable helping or auxiliary verb (is/am/are/was, etc.) The rules for using auxiliary verbs in passive voice sentences are different for each other.

Example:

The new published book is written by Ariel.

About the Author

Ariel C. Cabasag, LPT, MATELL

Ariel has been working as an English instructor and creative writer for almost six years in the Philippines. He's a man who loves letters and language, which really helps me to transform his imagination through creative writing. To him, life is meaningful and worthwhile, as he has expressed himself through writing such masterpieces in English literature.

In addition to that, he's famous insttuctor in teaching English communication, which further drives him to showcase his talents in poetry and essay writing. Most of his students was really inspired by his talents; indeed, he has received many appreciation letters in teaching.

With regards to his educational background, he took MA in Teaching English Language and Literature at Ateneo University, where he further learned the language. And got idolized some effective professors, who indeed motivated him to love teaching English language. After a year, he became a professor at Far Eastern University, where he published many poems: green letters in the cave and whisle in the milky way. Meanwhile, he started his second MA in Literary and Cultural Studies at Ateneo de Manila, where he further enhanced his talents in writing: to become globally competive both writing career and teaching.

www.ingramcontent.com/pod-product-compliance
Lightning Source LLC
LaVergne TN
LVHW041557070526
838199LV00046B/2016